W9-AVY-493

362.7
SCH

Schwartz, Perry.

Carolyn's story.

$21.27

3800300012774Z
12/09/1999

DATE			

C. A. FARLEY SCHOOL
119 COTTAGE STREET
HUDSON, MA 01749

BAKER & TAYLOR

A Book about an ADOPTED GIRL

Carolyn's Story

*Text and photographs
by Perry Schwartz*

LERNER PUBLICATIONS COMPANY / MINNEAPOLIS

Illustrations by John Erste

Copyright © 1996 by Lerner Publications Company

All rights reserved. International copyright secured. No part of this book
may be reproduced or transmitted in any form or by any means, electronic
or mechanical, including photocopying and recording, or by any
information storage or retrieval system, without permission in writing from
Lerner Publications Company, except for the inclusion of brief quotations
in an acknowledged review.

LIBRARY OF CONGRESS CATALOGING-IN-PUBLICATION DATA

Schwartz, Perry.
    Carolyn's story : a book about an adopted girl / text and
photographs by Perry Schwartz.
        p. cm.
    Includes bibliographical references.
    Summary: A nine-year-old girl describes her life and her feelings about
being adopted as a baby in Honduras. Includes information and
resources about adoption.
    ISBN 0–8225–2580–1 (alk. paper)
    1. Adopted children—United States—Case studies—Juvenile
literature. 2. Adoption—United States—Case studies—Juvenile
literature. [1. Adoption. 2. Intercountry adoption. 3. Honduran
Americans.] I. Title.
HV875.55.S38   1996
362.7'34—dc20   96–11188

Manufactured in the United States of America
1 2 3 4 5 6 JR 01 00 99 98 97 96

This book is dedicated to Mary Jane,
whose love has made us a family.

Legacy of an Adopted Child

Once there were two women
Who never knew each other.
One you do not remember;
The other you call mother.

The first gave you life and
The second taught you to live in it.
The first gave you a need for love
And the second was there to give it.

One gave you emotions;
The other calmed your fears.
One saw your first sweet smile;
The other dried your tears.

And now you ask me through your tears
The age-old question through the years.
Heredity or environment—which are
you the product of?
Neither, my darling, neither.
Just two different kinds of love.

—*Anonymous*

AUTHOR'S NOTE TO PARENTS

The thoughts expressed in this book are those of my daughter, Carolyn. Understandably, she moves back and forth across a range of emotions: on one end, she's proud to be adopted, because it's different. She enjoys the attention (most of the time, at least). On the other side, Carolyn just wants to fit in—to be like everyone else.

My wife and I do not find this perplexing. Rather, we see it as part of Carolyn's journey toward understanding herself. Many of Carolyn's thoughts about adoption grew from the seeds we planted and continue to nurture.

Carolyn's place in our family is the result of a journey. As with most journeys, we encountered twists and turns, bumps and detours, along the way. For those interested in adoption as a means of creating a family, there is a wealth of books, tapes, support groups, and agencies concerned with adoption and adoption issues. In fact, there are so many choices that beginning the journey may seem like the most difficult step.

Children of all ages, ethnic backgrounds, and situations need parents. By some estimates, more than 100,000 children are waiting in the American foster care system alone.

For those who wonder whether a parent's love for an adopted child differs from his or her love for a birth child, the answer is clearly "no." Our feelings for Carolyn and her brother, Michael, are the same as those we have for my two birth children, Catherine and Elizabeth.

Parents, we believe, have two responsibilities to their children: to give them roots, and to give them wings. Carolyn is on her way. We wish her, and all children, Godspeed.

Perry Schwartz

CONTENTS

MY NAME IS CAROLYN, and I'm nine years old. I was born in Honduras, in Central America. When I was a baby, my parents adopted me. I have a brother, Michael, who is seven. He was also adopted from Honduras, two years after me. We don't have the same birth parents, but now we are a family.

I live in Minneapolis with my parents, my brother, and our cat, Coco. I also have two older sisters, two grandmothers, aunts, uncles, cousins, friends, and neighbors.

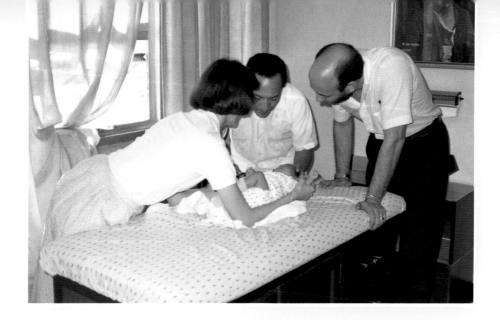

Mom and Dad traveled to Honduras to meet me when I was two months old. They got ready for my arrival the same way birth parents do, except they saw me for the first time in a hotel room instead of a hospital room. Mom says she was excited and nervous. She had never held her own little baby before. Dad has two older children, so he remembered what it was like.

I had to go to the hospital right away because of an ear infection. Mom and Dad lived in the hospital room with me, changing my diaper and feeding me, until I got better. That's the custom in Honduras.

I was adopted because my birth parents couldn't take care of me. They loved me and wanted me to be safe and healthy and happy. So they made a plan to find a good home for me.

My adoptive parents wanted to have a baby. They found out they couldn't have birth children, so they made a plan to adopt me. They worked with an adoption agency.

Adoption agencies bring together people who want to place a baby for adoption and people who want to adopt a child. There are many ways for an adoption to happen. Some adoption programs are in the United States. Other programs arrange for adoptions in foreign countries, such as Honduras.

The birth parents, the adoptive parents, and the adoption agency must obey many complicated rules and laws. Before my mom and dad could adopt me, they took tests and filled out lots of forms. Social workers visited their house and interviewed them.

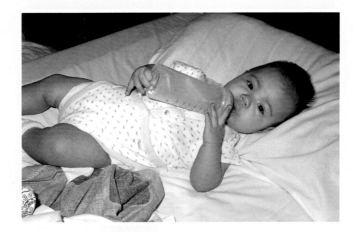

I DON'T MIND being adopted. I take piano lessons, ride my bike, go to school, play baseball, and watch TV. I like to swim, dance, play on the computer, and jump on the trampoline.

Being adopted means having two sets of parents: my birth mom and dad and my adoptive parents. That's special!

I have some questions that kids who are not adopted never ask. Like, are my birth mother and father still alive? Could I see them? I just want to say hi and see what they look like, where they live, and what it would have been like growing up in Honduras if they could have kept me.

Honduras is very far away from my home. When I'm older, my mom and dad say we can go back to Honduras to try to find my birth mother. I want to see the places I've only seen in pictures.

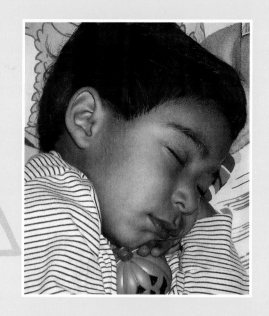

WHEN I WAS TWO YEARS OLD, Mom, Dad, and I went back to Honduras to meet Michael. He was only one week old. I remember eating chocolate pudding on the airplane and seeing Christina, my foster mother. She took care of me before Mom and Dad could bring me home.

Michael can be a pest, but he is nice, too. Boys can be obnoxious. Why do they bug you when they want your attention?

Being a big sister is hard. I have to keep an eye on my brother and be a helper to Mom and Dad. Michael asks me for help on things he can't do, like writing a capital "E" in cursive.

In our family we celebrate a special day. We call it "Gotcha Day." It's the day when Mom and Dad brought me and Michael home. I came home on March 25. Michael came home on March 23, two years later. So we picked a date for Gotcha Day that was in the middle—March 24.

Every Gotcha Day we get to do something fun. This year, we went to Chicago to visit my older sister Catherine, her husband, Eric, and their two cats. Dakota is the black cat. Sheba is white and brown.

Catherine is not adopted. She's my dad's daughter from before, when he was married to Catherine's mom. Catherine is a lot older than I am.

Mom and Dad stayed at a hotel. Michael and I stayed at Catherine and Eric's house. We all went downtown on the El (which is short for *el*evated train) and visited the Art Institute and Navy Pier. We took a boat ride on Lake Michigan.

I'm going to visit Catherine and Eric on my birthday, too. I get to ride on an airplane all by myself. Mom's worried, but I'm excited. Catherine will meet me at the airport in Chicago.

I'VE LEARNED that there are many ways to create a family. Adoption is just one way. An adoptive family is forever. My parents say that if your mom and dad take care of you and love you like a mom and dad, buy you clothes and treats like a mom and dad, and make sure you go to school like a mom and dad, then they are your mom and dad.

If I get sick, my parents take me to the doctor to help me get well. They buy me toys and books, tell me when it's time to go to bed, take me to the dentist and swimming lessons, and drive me to my friends' houses. I know my parents love me very much.

Some of my friends think that being adopted is a big deal. They think that not being adopted is boring! They're jealous because Superman was adopted and Robin, Batman's friend, was adopted, and Moses was adopted.

I have friends who are adopted, too. My friends Lily and Meagan were adopted from Korea. My friends Leah and Noah were adopted from Colombia. My friends Philip and Barbara were adopted from Honduras, like me. Elana, who lives across the street, was adopted from Paraguay.

My ancestors were European and Mayan. The Maya Indians lived in Honduras for thousands of years. Then the Spanish came looking for gold and treasure. They took over the land. Some of the Spanish people had children with the Maya. Many people in Honduras are a mixture of the two groups.

At my school, we have a rule about respecting others. Some kids don't obey that rule. On the playground they call me names. It's not because I'm adopted. It's because I look different from them. I have darker skin and hair.

A lot of people ask me, "Where did you come from? Where were you born?" I usually ask, "Why do you want to know?" If they have a good reason, and I think they're not trying to make fun of me, I might tell them. I'm getting better at handling those questions, but it's hard. Mostly, I ignore them.

Once my family was on vacation with my friend Meagan. She was born in Korea. While we were playing, a kid came up and said, "Where are you from, China?" It made me mad. Why should it matter?

Some kids are white, some black, some are like me. So what? Everybody's different.

Mariel and Jessica and Katie aren't adopted, and they're my friends. They don't treat me like I'm different. They just like me for who I am. We talk and play together.

I hate when my friends talk a lot about adoption. It makes me feel weird. Sometimes I don't like feeling special because I'm adopted. Most of the time I don't think about it much. I think about my friends, what I'm doing in school, and what's for dinner.

MOM AND DAD want me to know about Honduras. Every summer Michael and I go to a camp for kids adopted from Latin America. It's called La Semana [lah say-MAH-nah]. It means "The Week" in Spanish.

At La Semana we learn about the people, music, food, crafts, and languages of Latin America (Central and South America and Mexico.) This summer we learned about Brazil. The kids in my class made Carnival masks. Mine is a cat, and it looks just like Coco.

Carnival is a very important time in Latin America. Carnival means "farewell to meat." It takes place just before

Lent, the 40 days before Easter, when Catholics often stop eating meat. Days and nights during Carnival are filled with dancing, music, parties, and special foods.

The biggest Carnival festival in the world is in Rio de Janeiro [REE-oh dee ZHA-nair-oh], Brazil. Masquerades—parades where people wear masks—have always been part of Carnival. That's why we made masks at La Semana.

At La Semana, almost everyone looks like me—black hair, dark eyes, and coffee-with-cream colored skin. It takes me a while to get used to seeing so many people who look like me. It's hard to feel special when you look like everyone else.

The kids at camp are nice, but I don't really know many of them. It's fun to see them for a week. At the end of the week, we have a fiesta for all the families and perform Latin American dances.

I plan to join the La Semana dance troupe next year and perform at the Festival of Nations. The Festival of Nations is a fair where people from all over the world share dances, art, and food from their countries. When I'm in seventh grade, I want to be a volunteer at La Semana.

AT SCHOOL WE'RE STUDYING different countries. Everyone had to choose a country to share with the class. Most people picked a country they had never been to. All they knew about it was what they learned in the library.

I chose Honduras. I have a lot of interesting things from Honduras that Mom and Dad have saved for me. I showed the class my passport from Honduras, money, pictures, a doll, and books. We even sang "Head, Shoulders, Knees and Toes" in Spanish. Dad made flash cards with the words to the song on the computer.

My favorite subject in school is French. Mom and Dad also want me to learn Spanish, since that's what people speak in Honduras. I know a few Spanish words. My name in Spanish is Carolína [cahr-oh-LEE-nah]. Michael's is Miguel [Mee-GELL]. I like how the names sound in Spanish.

I LIKE SWIMMING, riding my bike, and collecting pogs, books, paper clips, and earrings. I spend most of the summer in our swimming pool. I can walk on my hands on the bottom, dive in the deep end, and do somersaults. I like to have friends over to swim.

Michael and I went fishing this summer. Dad taught me how to cast. At first, the hook kept getting caught in a tree. Finally, I threw the fishing line out really far. Then I caught a fish!

I also learned to play softball this summer. Our team came in second and we got a trophy. Everyone got to play all the positions. Being the catcher is fun, but sometimes the ball hit me in the head or got stuck in the mask.

Mom has a camera she's letting me use. I take pictures of the flowers in our garden and other things I like. Dad and I went to a rose garden to take pictures, and a wedding party was there. I took a picture of them getting their picture taken, and Dad took a picture of me taking their picture!

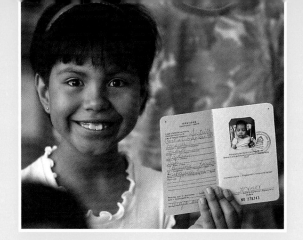

WHEN I GROW UP, I'll probably get married. And I'm probably going to adopt my children. Giving birth sounds like it hurts a lot. I'm not sure I want to have a birth child.

My dad told the social workers in Honduras that he wanted me to grow up to be president of the United States. They told him I can't be president because I wasn't born in the United States. Dad was surprised that people in Honduras knew so much about the United States.

I am an American citizen. Mom and Dad took me to a ceremony called "naturalization," where people who are not born in the United States become citizens. The judge gave Mom and Dad a beautiful certificate with my name on it. It says that I am an American citizen. Now I'm just like any American kid.

Information about **ADOPTION**

Adoption is one of many ways families are created. As in any family, adoptive children and their parents live together and love and support each other. Unlike a birth family, though, an adoptive family depends on the availability of children to adopt and adults to adopt them.

There are many reasons children are available for adoption. A child may be born into a home where the birth parents are very poor—so poor they cannot provide food, clothes, or a bed for the child.

Some children lose their birth parents through an accident or illness and have no one else in their family, such as uncles or aunts, who can take care of them. Other children have medical needs that their birth parents cannot manage.

Birth parents who cannot care for their child, or who choose not to raise the child, make plans for adoption in the hope that the child will grow up in a home where parents can take care of the child.

Many people find it difficult to understand how birth parents can place a child for adoption, allowing them to live with someone else. Sometimes parents have to make difficult and painful decisions. They think about what is best for the child—even if it makes the adults very sad.

Some children are abused, or badly hurt, by their parents. The government sometimes steps in to protect these children. The government often places abused children in foster homes (temporary places to live) until their family situation improves, or they may be placed for adoption (which is permanent).

There also are many reasons why people want to adopt children. Some married couples are not able to conceive a child. Other people have a medical condition or genetic disorder that they do not want to pass on to a child.

Some single women and men choose to adopt a child. Some people choose to adopt the child of a relative who has died. Others marry someone who already has children and choose to adopt those children.

Are adopted kids unique? Yes, just as every person is unique. Are adopted kids different? No more different or special than other kids. Adopted kids want to belong. They want to be loved. They want to do well in school—just like everyone else.

Adopted kids have some special challenges. For example, sometimes it's hard for an adopted kid to do a class assignment on family trees, because information about birth relatives may be missing or incomplete. Adopted kids, especially those of a different ethnic origin than their adopted family, rarely hear a family member say, "He looks just like Uncle Fred."

Sometimes adopted kids get asked questions like "Is that your real brother?" They might reply, "He isn't fake!" If someone asks an adopted kid, "Why don't you look like your mom or dad?" he or she might say, "Why is that information important to you?"

Adoption, like other areas of family life, is personal. Most people are willing to share personal information with people they trust.

If you know someone who is adopted, you can ask questions in a way that shows respect for your friend. The glossary of adoption terms will help you ask—and answer—questions about adoption with words that show respect for the person.

GLOSSARY

adoption (uh-DOP-shun) — a way to create a family by legally raising a child born to other parents. Children may be placed for adoption and adopted in many different ways. *See also* agency adoption, independent adoption, open adoption, traditional adoption.

adoption agency — a social service organization that brings together people who want to place a child for adoption and people who want to adopt a child

adoptive parents — the people who raise a child born to other parents

agency adoption — an adoption arranged by public (government) or private (religious or nonprofit) agencies

birth parents — a child's biological parents: the man and woman who conceived the child and passed on their genetic traits

conceive (kun-SEEVE) — to become pregnant

foster home — a temporary home for a child who cannot live with his or her family

genetic (juh-NET-ick) — having to do with the traits that are passed on from one generation to the next

independent (private) adoption — an adoption in which adoptive parents work with a lawyer, physician, or someone else (not an adoption agency) to find a child

open adoption — the type of adoption in which there is communication between the adoptive family and the birth family. The amount of contact varies, depending on what the families want.

naturalization (NATCH-ur-uhl-ih-zay-shun) — the process of becoming a citizen of a nation other than one's country of birth

social worker—a person who works in the social service field, helping people get along in life

traditional adoption — the type of adoption in which there is no contact between the adoptive family and the birth parents during or after the adoption process

For Further READING

Banish, Roslyn, with Jennifer Jordon-Wong. *A Forever Family.* New York: HarperCollins, 1992.

Bloom, Suzanne. *A Family for Jamie: An Adoption Story.* New York: C.N. Potter, 1991.

Cole, Joanna. *How I Was Adopted: Samantha's Story.* New York: Morrow Junior Books, 1995.

Fowler, Susi Gregg. *When Joel Comes Home.* New York: Greenwillow Books, 1993.

Greenberg, Judith E., and Helen H. Carey. *Adopted*. New York: Franklin Watts, 1987.

Jenness, Aylette. *Families: A Celebration of Diversity, Commitment, and Love*. Boston: Houghton Mifflin, 1990.

Kraus, Joanna Halpert. *Tall Boy's Journey*. Minneapolis: Carolrhoda Books, 1992.

Krementz, Jill. *How It Feels to Be Adopted*. New York: Knopf, 1982.

Lifton, Betty Jean. *Tell Me a Real Adoption Story*. New York: Knopf, 1994.

Livingston, Carole. *Why Was I Adopted?* Seacaucus, N.J.: Lyle Stuart, 1978.

Miller, Kathryn Ann. *Did My First Mother Love Me? A Story for an Adopted Child*. Buena Park, CA: Morning Glory Press, 1994.

Pellegrini, Nina. *Families Are Different*. New York: Holiday House, 1991.

Rogers, Fred. *Let's Talk about It: Adoption*. New York: Putnam, 1995.

Rosenberg, Maxine B. *Growing Up Adopted*. New York: Bradbury Press, 1989.

Resources

Adoptive Families of America, 3333 Highway 100 North, Minneapolis, MN 55422. Phone (800) 372-3300 or (612) 535-4829. AFA provides assistance with and information about adoption to members of adoptive families and prospective adoptive families. AFA seeks to create opportunities for successful adoptive placement and to promote the health and welfare of children without permanent families.

The *National Adoption Information Clearinghouse* maintains the nation's most comprehensive library of adoption materials. Established by Congress in 1987, NAIC is a service of the Administration for Children, Youth and Families in the Department of Health and Human Services. It is operated under contract by Cygnus Corporation, 5640 Nicholson Lane, Suite 300, Rockville, MD 20852. Phone (301) 231-6512.

The *North American Council on Adoptable Children* (NACAC) operates the National Adoption Assistance Training, Resource and Information Network (NAATRIN), which compiles and provides adoption assistance materials on a state-by-state basis. Contact NAATRIN at 970 Raymond Avenue, Suite 106, St. Paul, MN 55114-1149. Phone (612) 644-3036. Hotline: (800) 470-6665.

The *Children, Youth and Family Consortium Electronic Clearinghouse,* based at the University of Minnesota, Minneapolis, is an electronic collection of information on many adoption topics. The National Adoption Information Clearinghouse Publications and Services Catalog is housed at the Consortium. Phone (612) 626-1212. E-mail (cyfcec@maroon.tc.umn.edu). The Consortium also has a home page on the World Wide Web (http://www.fsci.umn.cyfc/AdoptINFO.html).

Here is a brief list of other national organizations concerned with adoption.

American Adoption Congress
1000 Connecticut Avenue NW, Suite 9
Washington, DC 20036
(202) 483-3399

Children Awaiting Parents, Inc.
700 Exchange Street
Rochester, NY 14608
(716) 232-5110

Committee for Single Adoptive Parents, Inc.
P.O. Box 15084
Chevy Chase, MD 20825

National Adoption Center
1500 Walnut Street, Suite 701
Philadelphia, PA 19102
(800) TO-ADOPT or (215) 735-9988

National Adoption Foundation
100 Mill Plain Road, Third Floor
Danbury, CT 06811
(203) 791-3811

Resolve, Inc.
1310 Broadway
Somerville, MA 02144-1731
(617) 623-1156

The World Wide Web portion of the Internet has an abundance of adoption information. Annette Thompson, an adoption advocate, is one of many people who have compiled a list of web sites about adoption. She can be reached by e-mail at: annette@acm.org, and on the www at http://precious.org/others.html

Also, most of the online computer services have adoption sections, including: Adoption section on Prodigy (see the social issues bulletin board), Adoption section on CompuServe, and Adoption section on America Online.